Miep and the Most Famous Diary

The Woman Who Rescued ANNE FRANK'S DIARY

WRITTEN BY MEEG PINCUS

ILLUSTRATED BY JORDI SOLANO

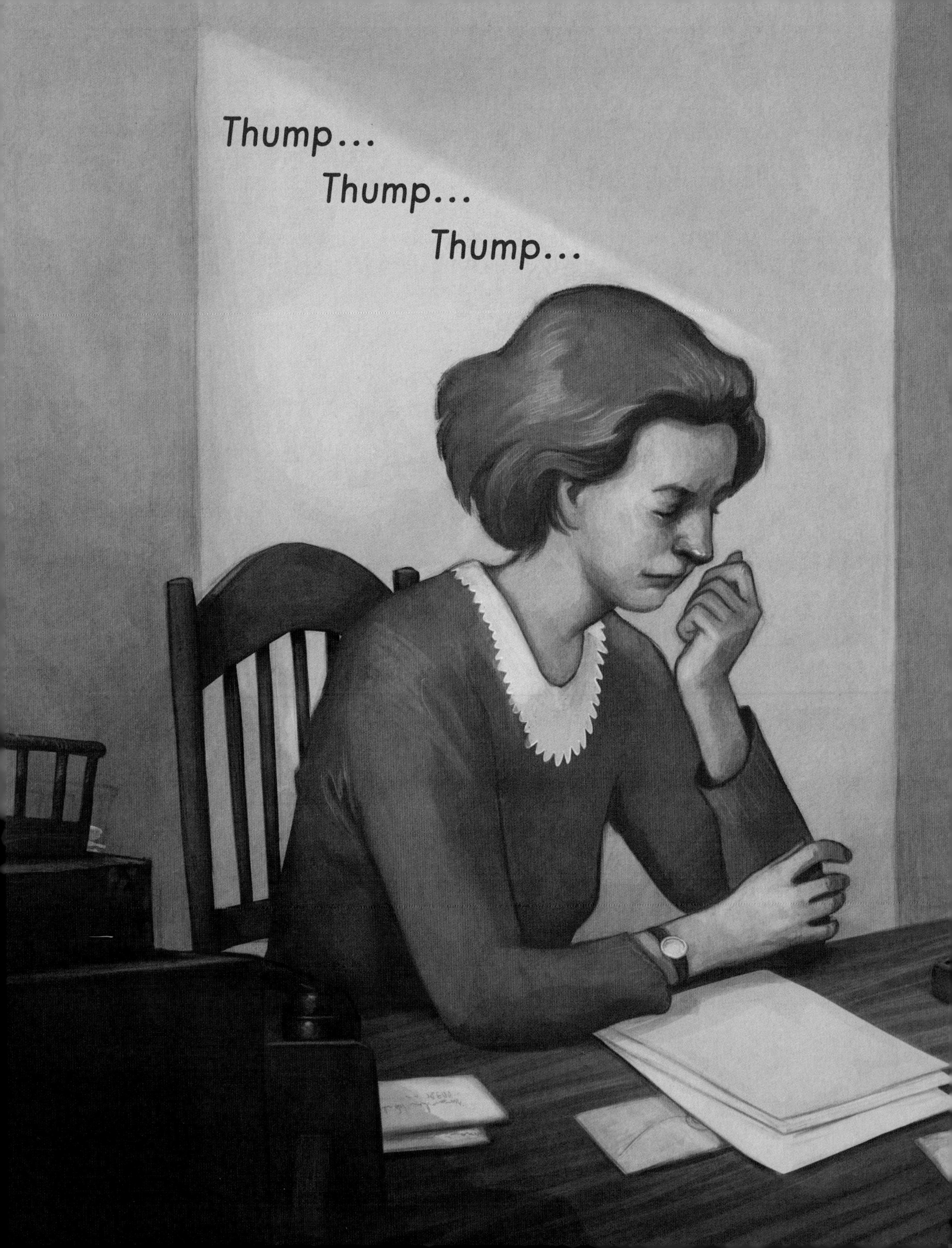

Thump...
Thump...
Thump...

Footsteps on the secret back stairs.

The worst sound Miep Gies has ever heard.

Worse than the World War II bomber planes buzzing over Amsterdam. Worse than the queen's quivering voice on the radio announcing the invading Nazi army.

Those footsteps are the worst-ever sound, on this, Miep's worst-ever day: August 4, 1944.

For they belong to Nazi officers... here to arrest the eight friends Miep has been hiding away in office storage rooms for two whole years.

Miep opposes the Nazis, who want to rid Europe of anyone different from them, especially Jewish people. Brave Miep is devoted to protecting those who are targeted—even though it puts her in danger as well.

One Nazi officer approaches Miep's desk, snarling like an angry bulldog.

"Now it's your turn," he growls, ready to arrest her.

But Miep's friends need her here to protect their business. And she hears something that might save her: the Nazi's accent reveals that they are from the same far-off hometown.

"I am from Vienna, too," she says, looking into his eyes.

He jerks back his head, paces, shouts. Then he leans in, his hot breath on her face.

"What shall I do with you?!" he barks. Miep stands strong.

"From me personally, you can stay," he says softly. Then loudly, "I'll be back to check on you. One wrong move and off you go to prison, too!"

As the Nazi officer leaves, slamming the door behind him, Miep thinks of her friends upstairs. Closest to her heart is her boss of eleven years, Mr. Frank, and his wife and two daughters. Miep has watched their youngest—Anne Frank— grow up, from toddler to teenager, and loves her dearly.

Just this morning, Miep had visited "the secret annex"—as Anne named the hiding place. Anne had tossed aside the checkered diary she's always writing in, greeting Miep with eager eyes and curious questions.

As usual, Miep had come for the morning grocery list. She crisscrosses Amsterdam daily, cautious as a cat, shopping for eight amid food shortages and suspicious soldiers. But now, no more meals will be eaten in the secret annex . . .

Instead, Miep's Jewish friends—and two coworkers who'd also helped them—are led into a Nazi police van.

Surely they will be sent to the cruel Nazi prison camps.
Miep nearly chokes at the thought.

Screeeech!

The van tears off down the street. They are gone.

Miep sits alone, still as a statue, barely breathing.

She knows the Nazis will send movers to take her friends' possessions—their furniture, jewelry, dishes, everything. The Nazis steal it all for themselves—and arrest those who keep any captured Jews' belongings.

There is one item, though, that Miep must save. It calls silently from the musty rooms above.

Yet, she cannot bring herself to budge.

Tick.   Tick.   Tick.

The clock echoes in the empty office. Hours have passed since the Nazis left and still Miep has not moved.

But, when her husband, Henk, arrives with a coworker, Elli, Miep snaps back into action. She climbs up to the secret annex with them.

Miep cringes at the sight of her friends' belongings, toppled and strewn about. Then she dashes into the Franks' bedroom and spots it: young Anne Frank's diary, on the floor.

She pictures Anne leaning over her cherished diary, her hair skimming its pages. She knows Anne dreams of publishing it as a book after the war. It has been Anne's paper friend, her lifeline, during two lonely years in hiding.

Grasping the checkered book in her shaking hands, Miep urges Elli to help pick up the loose pages of Anne's scrawling handwriting scattered across the floor.

They should not risk taking anything else. But Miep grabs one more item: Anne's delicate combing shawl, strands of her dark hair clinging to its fabric like silky noodles.

Ba-bum-ba-bum-ba-bum.

Miep's heartbeat pounds inside her ears like a motor as she rushes down the stairs to her desk.

She shoves the diary, papers, and shawl into a drawer and slams it shut.

When the Nazis' movers come to take her friends' belongings, Miep sits frozen in place. Anne's items hide in the drawer beside her.

She lets out her breath when the movers leave. She has rescued the diary. She will not read it—of course not. It belongs to Anne. And she will save it for Anne to publish after the war.

Miep clings to one hope in that dark, dismal time:
Anne's return.

Whoosh!!

Henk flings open their apartment door, the wind at his back.
It has been nine months since their friends' arrest—awful months
of wartime hunger, sadness, and fear.

"Miep, I have good news for you," Henk says. "The war is over!"

The Nazis have surrendered.

Miep and Henk wait for weeks, for rescuers' planes to bring food,
for friends and neighbors to return from the camps. Some people
trickle back into town, skinny as skeletons, with nothing but the
soiled Nazi camp uniforms on their backs.

Will the Frank family be among them?

Miep looks out their apartment window one afternoon. *Could it be?* Mr. Frank himself trudges up to their front door, looking as frail and dazed as an injured bird.

Miep's eyes glisten with tears of relief. But her heart drops when Mr. Frank speaks. His wife is not coming back, he says. She died of illness and starvation in the camp.

He holds hope for Anne and her sister, though. Sent to another camp, they'd still been healthy enough to work the hard labor the Nazis demanded.

Miep provides Mr. Frank a room and nurses him back to health and work. A wordless waiting joins them at the office, as Mr. Frank writes desperate letters searching for his daughters.

Sssssshhhhhhhhhhp.

Sorting mail, Mr. Frank slices open a letter. This becomes the second-worst sound Miep has ever heard.

For the letter contains the worst possible news: Anne and her sister did not survive the war. Illness took them just two months before the Nazi surrender.

The air in the office hangs as still and shattered as the day of the capture.

Miep sits stunned, sick from the shock of her one hope . . . lost.

Miep opens her desk drawer and gathers Anne's diary, papers, and shawl in her trembling hands once again. She has not touched them since she placed them there on that dreadful day many months ago.

Handing them to Mr. Frank, she says, "This is what Anne has left."

Mr. Frank gasps. He had given Anne the little diary three years earlier on her birthday, just before the family slipped into hiding.

His knees nearly buckle as he takes the precious items to his private office.

Flip flip flip.

Mr. Frank turns each page of Anne's diary, reading every word over the next few months. He savors her tales of growing up in hiding, her bright calls for hope when all seems lost.

"Miep, you must read Anne's writing!" he says. "Who would have imagined what went on in her quick little mind?"

Miep shakes her head and turns away. She refuses to read it each time he asks. She has pushed her tears down so deep inside, if they surface she will surely drown in sorrow.

Mr. Frank shows the diary to a fellow survivor of the camps, who shows it to a war historian, who persuades Mr. Frank to publish it as a book. Anne becomes the author she had always wished to be.

But, even as Anne's book is published worldwide, Miep still cannot bear to read it.

Click!

Miep closes the door of her room. After years of refusing, she is finally ready. She must be completely alone to read Anne's diary.

Her chest and jaw squeezed in tight knots, she opens to the first page. Then she reads . . . all of it in one sitting.

Anne's voice—such a sweet, familiar sound—fills Miep's head, as if Anne is standing right beside her, chattering away. No longer gone, but alive and well, Anne shares her youthful moods, lively stories, and inspiring ideals.

"*I want to go on living even after my death!*" says Anne, her voice ringing clear from the page. "*And therefore I am grateful [for] this gift…of writing, of expressing all that is in me.*"

Almost two years to the day of living in hiding, Anne proclaims: "*In spite of everything, I still believe people are good at heart.*"

Reading Anne's words, hearing her voice again, Miep's chest and jaw unclench like surrendering fists. The ache in her heart eases.

She is holding one of the most famous books in the world. Anne Frank's diary is translated into many languages and treasured by millions of readers.

It dawns on Miep: because of the little checkered diary that she saved on that worst-ever day—August 4, 1944—her beloved Anne *will* live on and on.

Author's Note

As a girl, I read *The Diary of Anne Frank* over and over again, so much that I felt Anne was a friend. She had big feelings, Jewish heritage, and wanted to be a writer, just as I did. And I looked up to Miep Gies, Anne's protector, as a hero.

Then, as a young woman more than 20 years ago, I had the honor of meeting Miep in person. She was in the United States on a tour, and I was a newspaper reporter assigned to write a story about her talk at a local school. I've never forgotten her quiet, gentle strength or the love in her eyes when she spoke about Anne, 50 years after World War II.

I based this book on Miep's own autobiography, and every quote you read in this story is exactly as Miep remembered it in her book, speeches, or interviews. Other people's accounts about some details differ (for example, exactly how Mr. Frank learned about Anne's fate), and some of the action is condensed, but this story is based on how Miep remembered these events in her life and shared them.

I am honored to share Miep's story with today's children.

MORE ABOUT MIEP'S COURAGE

Miep lived to be 100 years old, until 2010, though she risked her life many times to help others and almost starved to death during both world wars. All five secret annex helpers survived World War II, but Mr. Frank was the only survivor of the eight hiders.

Of the day of the hiders' capture, August 4, 1944, Miep said 50 years later, "I have never overcome that shock." For the rest of her life, every August 4th she closed the curtains, did not answer the phone, and had a day of mourning.

Miep's life story is defined by her courage and compassion. She and her husband, Henk, both risked their lives daily to help friends and strangers who were threatened by the Nazis. (By the way, Henk's real name was Jan, but Anne changed all the names for her diary except Miep's. In her own writing, Miep used Anne's made-up names, so I followed her lead.)

After the hiders were captured, Miep marched into the dangerous Nazi police headquarters twice and offered the officer from Vienna money to free them. Though he refused, Miep had the courage to try everything she could.

Miep and Anne's memories are preserved in the secret annex, which is now a museum: The Anne Frank House (visit online at www.annefrank.org). There, you can see Anne's original checkered diary, her combing shawl, and the place where Miep helped keep eight Jewish people hidden for two years under Nazi occupation.

But, Miep did not want to be viewed as a hero. "Imagine young people would grow up with the feeling that you have to be a hero to do your human duty," she said. "I am afraid nobody would ever help other people, because who is a hero? I was not."

Can you imagine the world if everyone followed this principle—if we all saw it as simply our human duty to help others in need, under any circumstances?

February 15, 1909
Miep is born in Vienna, Austria (birth name: Hermine Santruschitz).

1920
During World War I, she is starving and sick. To save her life, her parents send her to live in Amsterdam, the Netherlands, with a kind Dutch family, who nickname her Miep.

June 12, 1929
Anne Frank is born in Frankfurt, Germany.

January 1933
Adolf Hitler, the anti-Jewish Nazi leader, becomes chancellor of Germany.

Fall/Winter 1933
Miep begins working for Otto Frank, who has recently left Nazi Germany with his Jewish family.

May 10, 1940
The Nazi army invades the Netherlands. The queen and royal family flee, leaving the Dutch people under Nazi rule.

July 16, 1941
Miep marries Henk (Jan) Gies. Anne and her father attend their wedding at Amsterdam City Hall.

Spring 1942
All Jews in Holland are ordered to wear yellow Jewish stars above their hearts to identify themselves.

July 6, 1942
The Frank family goes into hiding in the secret annex, with help from Miep, Henk, and three other employees of Mr. Frank.

August 4, 1944
Nazi officers arrest the eight hiders in the secret annex and send them to a prison camp.

August 7 and 8, 1944
Miep enters the dangerous Nazi headquarters and tries to buy the hiders' freedom, twice, but is denied.

October 1944
Anne and her sister are separated from their parents and sent to a different camp.

Winter 1944–45
The Nazis cut off all food and supply transport to the Netherlands. Some 20,000 Dutch people die of starvation. Miep and Henk are desperately hungry.

January 6, 1945
Anne's mother dies in a Nazi camp of illness and starvation.

January 27, 1945
Allied soldiers liberate the Nazi camp where Mr. Frank is found near death. He gets care there before beginning his long journey back to Amsterdam.

February 15, 1945
On her 36th birthday and nearly starved, Miep risks her life to travel by bicycle to the countryside to find food for herself and Henk.

March 1945
Anne and her sister die of typhus (a deadly infection from lice bites) in a Nazi camp.

MIEP'S *Life*

May 7, 1945
The war on the European front is over, with Germany's surrender. Miep and Henk stay home in quiet reverence rather than join the streetwide celebrations.

June 3, 1945
Mr. Frank arrives at Miep and Henk's apartment. He moves in with them and continues living with them for seven years.

September 2, 1945
World War II officially ends.

June 25, 1947
Anne's diary is first published (as *The Secret Annex*) in the Netherlands.

July 13, 1950
At age 41, Miep gives birth to her only child, Paul.

1952
Anne Frank: The Diary of a Young Girl is first published in the United States, with an introduction by First Lady Eleanor Roosevelt.

April 16, 1959
Miep and the Netherlands' queen attend the opening of a Hollywood film about Anne's diary. Miep also attends the 1960 Academy Awards, where it's nominated for Best Picture.

May 3, 1960
The Anne Frank House opens to the public. The secret annex is now a museum of remembrance.

March 8, 1972
Miep and Henk are awarded the Yad Vashem medal of honor in Israel for their bravery in helping Jews during World War II.

August 19, 1980
Mr. Frank dies. Miep becomes the living ambassador of Anne Frank's legacy. She begins to tour the world.

May 15, 1987
Miep's autobiography is published. She is 78.

January 26, 1993
Miep's husband, Henk (Jan Gies), dies.

1994
Miep wins the Wallenberg Medal as an outstanding humanitarian. In her speech she says, "*I feel strongly that we should not wait for our political leaders to make this world a better place. No, we should make this happen now in our homes and at our schools.*"

January 11, 2010
Miep dies at age 100.

June 12, 2013
Miep Gies Park is dedicated in Amsterdam on the street where Miep and Henk lived—on what would have been Anne's 84th birthday.

2019
Anne's diary has been published in 70 languages. The Anne Frank House hosts 1.2 million visitors yearly, plus millions more online, and has educational programs in over 70 countries. Anne—and Miep—live on and on.

For a full bibliography and educational guide, please visit sleepingbearpress.com/teaching_guides.

For J. David Pincus, who taught me about resilience, the joy of the writing life,
and the importance of honoring our history. Thanks, Dad.

And for all the helpers who, like Miep, act with compassion and courage,
no matter the circumstances.

—Meeg Pincus

✂

To Miep Gies. To all who dared to stand up against evil, injustice, and
oppression back then. To all who will stand up and not let it happen again.
Mai més. Enlloc. Contra ningú.

—Jordi Solano

Sleeping Bear Press®
2395 South Huron Parkway, Suite 200
Ann Arbor, MI 48104
www.sleepingbearpress.com

Printed and bound in the United States.

10 9 8 7 6 5 4 3 2

Library of Congress Cataloging-in-Publication Data

Names: Pincus, Meeg, author. | Solano, Jordi, illustrator.
Title: Miep and the most famous diary : the woman who rescued Anne Frank's
diary / by Meeg Pincus ; illustrated by Jordi Solano.
Description: Ann Arbor, MI : Sleeping Bear Press, [2019] | Ages 6-10. |
Summary: When the Frank family and others are found and arrested during
World War II, Miep Gies hides young Anne's papers from the Nazis and later
is instrumental in having her beloved friend's diary published.
Identifiers: LCCN 2019010252 | ISBN 9781534110250 (hardcover)
Subjects: LCSH: Gies, Miep, 1909-2010—Juvenile nonfiction. | Frank, Anne,
1929-1945—Juvenile nonfiction. | CYAC: Gies, Miep, 1909-2010—Nonfiction. |
Frank, Anne, 1929-1945—Nonfiction. | Diaries—Nonfiction. | Courage—Nonfiction. |
Holocaust, Jewish (1939-1945)—Netherlands—Amsterdam—Nonfiction.
Classification: LCC PZ7.1.P557 Mie 2019 | DDC [E]—dc23
LC record available at https://lccn.loc.gov/2019010252